This book is dedicated in loving memory of my mom,
Nettie Lee Litzler,
who nurtured in me a love of books from an early age.

•

In addition to the fantastic illustrations by Constance Christensen,
the author gratefully acknowledges the graphic design work of
Akos Horvath and the administrative oversight of Wendy Mays
in bringing this book to life.

ISBN 979-8-9992219-0-2 *(Hardcover)*
ISBN 979-8-9992219-1-9 *(Paperback)*
ISBN 979-8-9992219-2-6 *(Digital)*

•

If You Pick a Pair of Peacocks

James W. Litzler

·

Illustrated by
Constance Christensen

If you pick a pair of peacocks
And a pair of pesky parrots

And two fine and fancy *felines*

And two frisky furry *ferrets*.

Then you add two paunchy penguins

And two pandas and two snakes

And two happy heavy *hippos*

And a she *duck* and he *drake*.

Add two lumpy humpy camels

And two oozy woozy worms

With a pair of crocs and gators

And two skunks that make you squirm.

Then you build a boat that's taller
Than six giraffes stacked in a heap

And longer than a llama lands

In fifty lunging leaps.

If you nicely take precisely two
Of everything that growls
Or that hisses, crows or clucks
Or that hoots or honks or howls.

Add in those that chirp and chatter
Plus those that purr, meow, and bark
And you bring them all together
And you put them in your ark.

Then your name just might be Noah
Who God told to build the ark
And then fill it up with critters
That purr, meow and bark.

God picked Noah for a purpose
And He put him in a place
And He told him what his job was
And He filled him with His grace.

And then Noah got to cracking
Stacking wood to build the ark
Packing hay and food and water
Working every day past dark.

Never worried by the laughing
And the teasing and the kidding
From the folks who didn't realize
He was doing God's own bidding.

Noah built it, then God filled it

With His critters, two by two

Peacocks, parrots, cats and ferrets

Penguins, snakes and cockatoo.

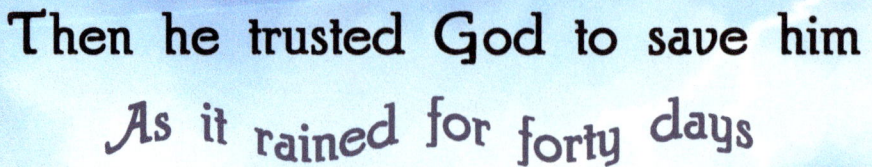

Then he trusted God to save him
As it rained for forty days

While inside he and his family
Slopped and mopped and hayed and ... prayed.

And when God dried up the *water*
And the ark was back on land

Noah set the critters free to go
Just as God had planned.

So when God gives you a purpose
And He puts you in a place
And He tells you what your job is
And He fills you with His grace.

Then you'd better get to cracking
On the job to do God's bidding
And don't worry if there's laughing
If there's teasing and some kidding.

As you do the job
God gave you
When He put YOU in your place.

About the Author

James is a bank attorney by profession.
He and his wife Janie live in Sulphur Springs, Texas.
The son of a Baptist minister and an English teacher,
James has known and loved the great stories of the Bible
since childhood and grew up appreciating the value of
a well-turned phrase. It's that love and appreciation
that he hopes to pass on to his own grandchildren
and to your children and grandchildren
through his books.

www.ingramcontent.com/pod-product-compliance
Lightning Source LLC
Chambersburg PA
CBHW040513150626
46551CB00033B/2636